Part of Me

Leslie J. Gruendl Tepper

Selected Journal Entries

Edited by Charlotte Gruendl

Copyright © 2018 by Charlotte Gruendl

All rights reserved. Printed in the United States of America. No part of this book may be used or reproduced in any manner whatsoever without written permission except in the case of brief quotations embodied in critical articles and reviews. For information, contact the author or publisher, Manzanita Writers Press.

ISBN 978-0-9968858-8-1

Manzanita Writers Press
manzapress.com
manzanitawp@gmail.com

Cover photo credit and interior photos:
    Gruendl Family Photo Collection
Layout Designer: Joyce Dedini
Additional Editing: Joy Roberts, MWP

Foreword

Our daughter Leslie was a precocious child. She was raised with four brothers, so she was a little bit of a tomboy. At the age of thirteen, she had to try everything, which she always managed to accomplish.

She was very bright and excelled in her schoolwork. After graduating from high school, it became difficult for her to decide what she wanted to pursue as a career. Finally, she decided that helping people would be her calling, so she chose clinical psychology. After receiving her Ph.D. and becoming a licensed psychologist, one of her many professional accomplishments includes Clinical Director at Fuller Theological Seminary Graduate School of Psychology.

I cannot begin to say how proud I was of her when I went on a trip with her to Washington, D.C. She was the featured speaker, and when they announced her name, *Dr. Leslie Tepper*, I nearly jumped out of my seat clapping.

She was published in the *Psychiatric Services* book, a journal of the American Psychiatric Association. She went on to receive another Ph.D. in psychoanalysis. After leaving Fuller, she opened a private practice in clinical psychology and psychoanalysis in Pasadena, California. She gave up her practice in 2013 when cancer prevented her from continuing with the work she loved. She passed away in 2014 with her parents at her side. It was far too soon–she had so much more to give.

Our daughter had a very successful career and accomplished many things in her lifetime. She was a very giving and kind person and left us a wonderful grandson and two beautiful great-grandchildren. Her father thinks about her every day and misses her, as do her four brothers. But only a mother knows that when you lose a child, your grieving never stops. She was a part of me.

Letter to Leslie

My Daughter,

What happens when a mother has a daughter? Is there a special bond created between them? I think so. I always knew when something was wrong, and you always seemed to know when things were not right with me.

You were a typical child, bright in school with many friends and always trying something new.

I'll never forget when I got a call from school saying you were doing somersaults on the bars in the school yard with your skirt flying. Please come and get her! When I picked you up, I was surprised that you and your friend had worn shorts under your skirts, so what was their problem? I thought that was very clever of you. You were eleven years old.

You took many years of ballet lessons, appeared in several Christmas pageants and also took singing lessons in your teens. Adagio came next, but that did not work. At one of your classes, I never laughed so hard when you had to jump, and your partner had to catch you. Well, he did somehow but staggered all over the floor trying to hold onto you while you were yelling, "Don't drop me!" I know it wasn't funny, but it sure looked funny. Anyway, that was the end of Adagio!

When you turned thirteen, I wanted to lock you up. You started hanging out after school in the park. On several occasions, you ran away, and off we would go to retrieve you. I would be so mad at you, as you had to push that last button and set me off. We always managed to find you and bring you home. I would grab you by your pony tail and pull. I wondered if that was the reason you kept your hair short as an adult.

Our doctor suggested a trip with just the three of us might help you to bond with your father. You were giving us a bad time and constantly arguing with your father. Well, we followed the doctor's advice and took off for a trip to England. We spent a couple of days in London, then rented a car and drove to the south and Brighton Beach. We stayed in Bed & Breakfasts along the way and had a glorious time. One morning you woke up to see a cow poking its head in your bedroom window.

We enjoyed tea on the beach, but it is still questionable if much bonding happened. I know you loved us both very much even though you were a rebellious teen.

There was only one incident, when we went to this very popular restaurant in London. We were kept waiting for a table for a long time, and we finally asked what the problem was. We were told we could not be seated because you were not "dressed appropriately." You wore a suede outfit that was a little skimpy on top, but very stylish at the time. We were finally seated, and I was shocked to see how dirty the Chef's apron was and thought—they complained about what *we* wore.

After grammar school we sent you to an all-girl's Catholic high school. Needless to say, you were there only six months before they asked you to leave. As parents we were determined to get you through high school, and at times it seemed unlikely. One never knows. As soon as you did graduate, off to Europe you went with a girlfriend. You hitchhiked all over Europe and worked along the way to help with expenses. One of my happiest moments was when you called from Switzerland and yelled, "Mom, it's just like Heidi! I'm standing on a mountain!" You were so excited. *Heidi* and *Peter and the Wolf* were two of your favorite books as a child. The trip lasted almost a month, and that was enough—it was time to come home and start your next chapter.

The time came to decide what you wanted to do for a career. Your first choice was acting, so we sent your portfolio off to the Lee Strasberg Theater and Film Institute in Los Angeles. After a few lessons, you appeared in *Godspell,* but you had had enough. Your analysis was that acting is a plastic world that you wanted no part of. Next came dog training, and again that did not do it for you. You felt that the dogs' owners were the ones who needed training.

This was a period when you held many different jobs to pay for expenses while living in Los Angeles. Oftentimes you held two jobs, waitressing and selling tickets in a theatre. Soon you realized that psychology was to be your field. After many years of school and work to support yourself, you had another accomplishment—our first grandchild, a beautiful baby boy.

We went through a lot together, and you were close to your father and brothers as you grew up. As an adult, you achieved so much, and you left us with many cherished memories.

Love,

Your mother,
Charlotte Gruendl

To my beloved grandchildren,

Alie & Matthew

Love

Where is his feather, when you need it, my love is caring for me and
turns the sand of the desert in the gentlest of ways.
My breasts swell as in the swells of waves, but then,
when I really think about it . . . I hear a snip and then my breasts
shall match the depth of my love for him.

We are back, but all too slowly . . . am I up to the challenge?
I love him so yet he is, well, it seems, more scared than me!
Can I be patient and see his side?
I must detach and get healthy now in order to let my old self blossom
and allow true caring and the brightness of love emerge.

There is a man . . .
I touch him as much as I can to make sure he is real.
It seems that now, I may continue to drown in his kindness.
He says he thinks of me . . .
Ah . . . but to drown in the kindness of men.

The cycle continues—
Am I that obnoxious?
Will someone love me?
What am I afraid of?
The adolescent rebellion maybe rebels further.

He always chooses not to understand.
His defensiveness makes me needy and scared.
Why does he need to protect himself so.
He loses the fluidity in life. He misses out.
Who hurt him?
Who betrayed him?
Why is he so scared?
I wish he had these insights.
I wish he could share them with me.

A rented room, an unmade bed.
For that one night love was given freely,
beautifully and more in one night than you gave
me in a year.

Year Three

To know the crevice of my olive spine, dangle down, flesh
made curving, sliding intertwined.
To know the crease of hidden 'hind knees, tickle lines cry,
sing out, screaming high and free.
To know my nape as a place, to dip, to dive, swirly down with
red, milky lips.
Take your time this year number three, to find my outside,
my soul made flesh for your precious hand, carefree.
Celebrate with me the power of the bond, of the essence of
succumbing too long . . . the long winding, swirly road to love.

On being sensuous—
Many men feel that on being sensuous,
the woman has no say.
And that she is absurd if involvement means one must pay.
Also the value of her love is as noticeable as night
turning into day.
Well, I must protest on being sensuous.
That the sensuous woman could be described as luscious.
Also, as I mentioned, the male's opinion on the matter
is quite discourteous.
And if you ask my personal opinion, the male's penis is
quite hideous.

My search . . . amidst the thick shrubs. Be careful, they
are dangerous.
One careless puncture and the poisonous juices will
devour my blood.
I can see light on the other side—my destiny.
Searching for the way out, out of this confusion and frustration.
Protect me, Great Spirit.
My life wants to be at its fullest.
This can only happen once I feel the white feathering
heat of the brilliant light in the distance.
Colors of mauve and lavender form transparent filters
over my vision.
I can see only vaguely.
Future scenes never to be predicted
It is forbidden—they are foggy.
Past experience washed out to a faded grey
descending to the bottom of consciousness.
Now the present—forever grasping it
moment to moment
trying to make it as real as possible.
Hold fast.
These present moments mold the future
and create the past behind you.
My search for love. How common to talk or write about it.
How can I make my experience different.
Enjoy the search—
be happy with every partner 'til departing.

Pale pink satin
a light cool breeze.
Come on down, let it
loose, with a little ease.

Red, red roses,
fragrances bestow content.
Come lie beside me,
your love makes soft relent.

Smooth silk skin
soft brown eyes
Come take me in your
soul of soft pale blue skies.

Of greed and passion
were the songs we sang.
Come close to kiss me.
Let me taste your soft
warm tongue.

I am proud to say, though, you cannot hurt me.
I cannot hurt you.
I loved only your company and cared for only your presence.
We do not realize one another's souls . . . and we hurt.

You know, I'm tired,
I'm tired of people hurting each other.
I'm tired of not knowing why.
I'm tired of your pretending you don't know me.
I'm tired of wondering.
I'm tired of hurting.
I'm tired of being hurt.
But most of all, I'm tired of crying inside . . .
We know men's faces, not their minds.

Faith

Things have happened so radically—will my luck run out or is
this feeling a remnant of the low self-esteem that
keeps me strapped to the dark side?
Be Still
I get busy—I lose touch with my faith—that ever-holding,
all-encompassing feeling and sensation that God has kept me warm
safe and secure all along.
Now, then, and forever.
Be Still
The surge begins—from my toes, to my gut, through my heart
and settles in my mind.
Faith—I am centered again.

I'm preparing soulfully for work tomorrow. It feels good to
do a little soul writing. I love my work. I thank you, God,
for allowing me to help others. Keep my art focused and
passionate. Help me to find the jewels in others.
Help me to help them locate and love their souls.

Lift my anxiety from the hours in which I need sleep
and place it into words—
Talk about it.
Pray about the anxiety.
This week is for me
I need rest—
I need your spirit to ease my anxiety—Now.

Can I ever
Oh God, will I ever
feel the warmth?
Please will I ever
 I give up, will I ever
feel the smoothness.

I don't feel like
explaining anymore.
I don't know who
I'm talking to,
or whose warmth
and smoothness
I'm referring to
but I think I've
known it in my dreams.

P.S. Are dreams really
only for those who sleep?

Intervals between entries are huge and getting bigger.
What happened to the spirit of the young girl who
trampled through the redwoods?
The crunch-crunch of pine needles beneath my feet.
Leaping onto rocks that are altars.
I perched, looked about and talked to God.
God . . . stretch my soul.
Moreover, stretch my arms, so that I can
reach way down into my corpus
and pull it out.
Pull it out—help me to wash it clean, give it a little sun.
Give it a pep talk and a nice warm snuggle from Cookie.
I want my soul back, dammit—It's mine!
It doesn't belong to the insufferable
blistering salty tears of the recent past.
It has healed—so it needs to make an appearance.
Then spend a few days in the desert,
then meet with the God of the Sun
and mingle with the Fathers of the Desert.
Then back, back to God's work—
my work rejuvenated.

The straight life . . . I want it, I deserve to be loved.
I deserve to be trusted.
I deserve to be free.
I deserve to be respected.
Help me, God, guide me to that path . . .
Friends.
Health—sleep.
Sierra Club.
Psychology work—relations.
Celebration.
I am licensed—Thank you, God.
Spirituality

Scorched and tired, I love the exhaustion.
His presence in nature, on the trail,
that comes upon me.
These are the days that hold me together,
that allow me to experience that everything is OK.
Let me not say "for now though,"
Give me faith.
Not only to savor these days, but to take them, digest them,
sending them through the blood, the veins,
the organs of my body and mind.
Fueling me for all tomorrows.

Give me focus and strength.
No God jar.
Give it to me directly.
I have this right?
Absolutely. Therefore . . .
Give me focus and
strength,
swiftness of memory
and thought.
Allow me to analyze
clearly, concisely
freedom to go into
my mind and
retrieve information
randomly and
spontaneously.
No fancy tricks . . .
I need a clear mind,
head and heart.

I'm trying . . . trying.
My patients give me
courage.

I feel so ill . . . I want to
be better.

I feel so anxious . . . yet I
have some time.
Help me stay in gratitude.
Help me find the way.

Scared but faithful,
thank you, dreamworld.

There are angels
out there and some
are on my side.

I sense my health
and my commitment
to work appealing
to their prayers.

I want to ride on
their wings and wear
a loose garment as
we fly high over the . . .
fly high over
the obsessive
moody worries of the day

God, give me strength to
fly for me, for my son
and for my place in
the world.
And for today—
just for today
I am grateful
for
the courage to let you
in
the strength of heart
to love my art,
my work.
The openness to bridge
the distance—with piercing eye to
eye with others.

Just Me

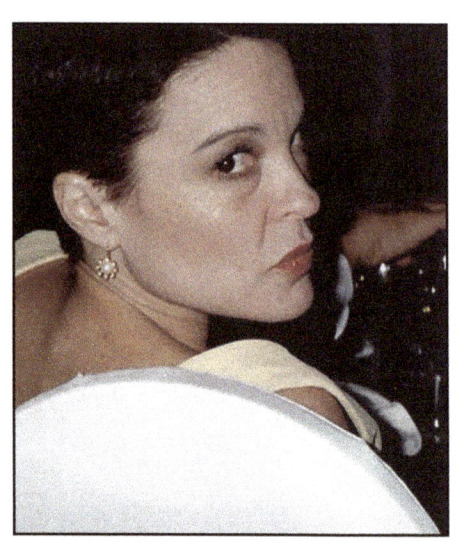

Inspiration comes and goes . . .
Aspiration for 1993 to stay in gratitude.
Remain filled with your guidance and love.
Become available to others—laughter, love, security, rhythm.

These recent days have been confusing,
disorienting and amalgamous.
They drive me back, then they drive me forward.
They send me in circles, lift me, turn me around and
place me in front of the mirror.
I pause . . . I look . . . I'm still here.

My only red rose is bleeding.
Barely able to struggle,
my rose gasps for a
sigh of relief
the moment death struck
gently.
As I held my rose,
dead it did not seem.
For her fragrance still
lingered and her
color still radiant.

Tootsie rolls, lemonade with seltzer,
and one more cigarette.
Cookie at my feet, waiting patiently
to attack my moving pen. Bright-eyed,
full of kitty wonder, kitty love.
Funny and frantic.

I was afraid of myself and it was just that simple.
My back sweaty yet cold, went flush against the brown
linoleum floor. I had to hold my head. It hurt.
It was my soul that, however, came jumping from below and
hit me hard. How was I going to function tomorrow?

A little cowboy appeared. His nervous sparkle is encouraging.
He is a lover, a member of the contemplative life. He will
be almost impossible to get close to. What a relief—I can
take my time without the garbage. Of course,
Alpine Texas is certainly the disturber. God help us both.
Two poets in cowboy hats
. . . a steadfast hand . . . and a graceful pen
will be the key to this friendship.
I wish and hope that the little cowboy from Texas
will be moved by my words, that my kindness will
appeal to his little Western heart.

To drown in the kindness of women, as per Woolf, is a wish
of one who yearns to be with women of like mind
and to allow others to follow, then
to allow is to let them grab, prod and poke
with no real or sliver of truth
and with no courage
to be straight forward and simply ask me—
ask me directly

I long to know . . . My funny smiles and hideous giggles can
only hold my bubbles before they burst.
I want to need . . . My childish babble and meaningless
stupidity can only last so long.
I have to feel . . . My quivering touch can be so gentle that
only I will find it through times of confusion.
I must learn . . . My thought of constant worry and split
emotion will teach me to be aware.

There was no time for soul searching now, I said.
How will I get my son to school?
I could then gear down and hold tight
to a bigger reality, keeping me afar.
A bigger reality—A bigger reality.

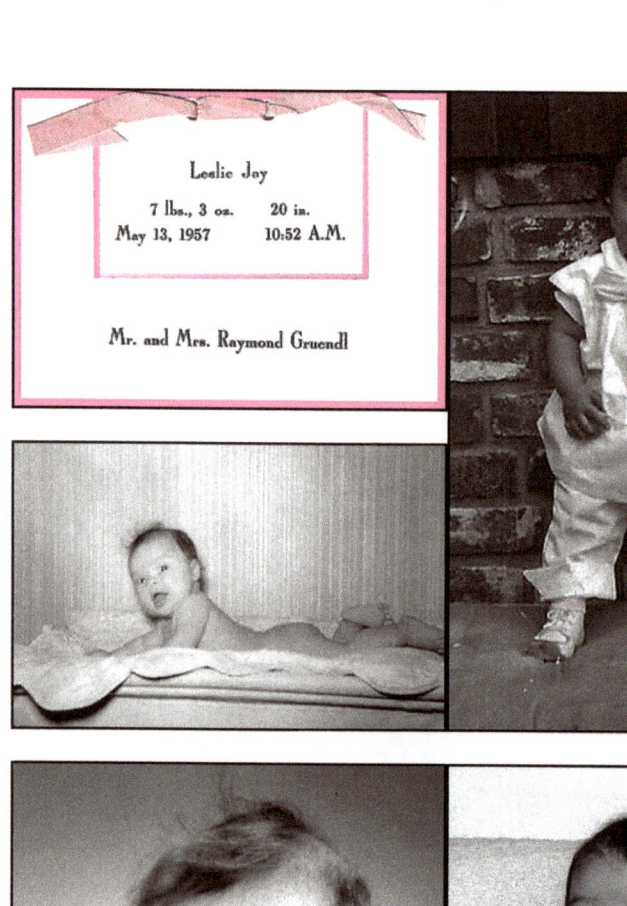
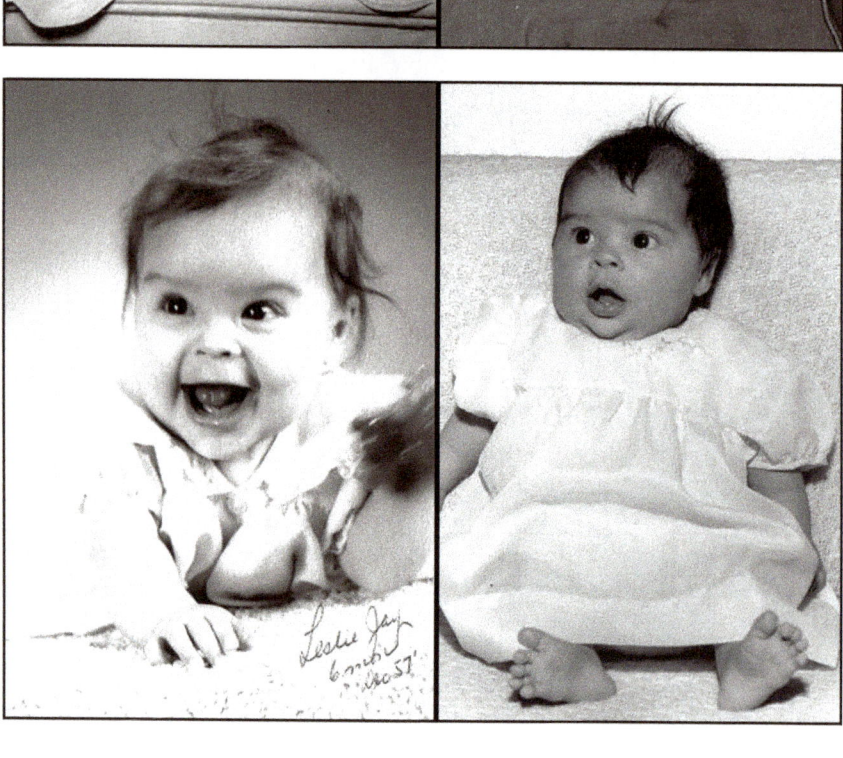

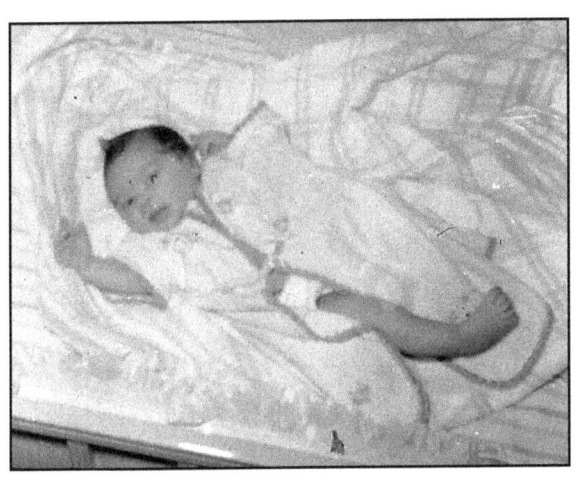

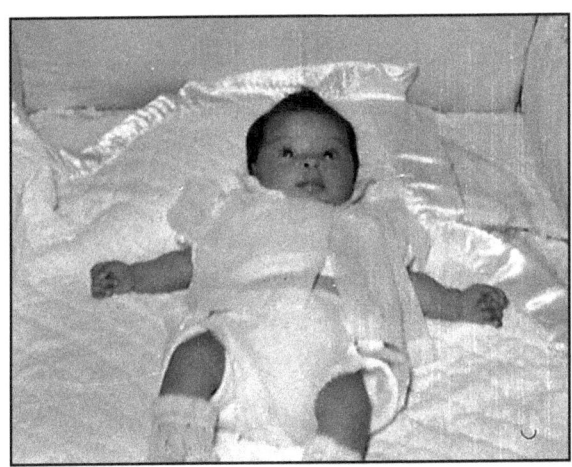

Full of energy
Ability to commit
Intuition
Trust my judgment
Higher power guide my act,
      my thoughts,
            and communication to others.

Now I am writing and it's eight years later, just like the long intervals between dental checks during my drinking years.
I looked though my earlier writings and am touched, moved by how vulnerable and how open I appeared. Now I am different on the outside at least. A peek into my internal world does not lack anything from those earlier times. But . . .

Such sorrow may dry drowning tears
I will not drown in vain.
My life, a web woven with goals will be vivid to me tomorrow in faint colors of mauve.
Joy, as a silkened laced petticoat flutters like a parasol in soft shades of pink.
Virtue in a gallant flow,
the horse rides deserts of burnt copper.
My love, was passion made passive as I vainly faded away in smooth feathered whiteness.

My cancer is something to befriend. I am getting to know
it in order to pave a smooth road to recovery.
Everyone says, "You're a fighter!"
One fights cancer?
Such adages employ research.
What despairing soul conjured
that up?
No, this is a peaceful family journey.
Maybe cancer comes
in like a lion,
but leaves like a lamb—
I'll make sure that's so.

I'm at peace with my status, my place in life.
I am back to the redwoods . . .
So I will work, work, work.
I will recreate, recreate, recreate.
I will love, love, love.
I will be grateful each day for my art,
for my son,
my life in the redwoods,
 my soul in the redwoods with God.
With God . . . talking . . .
learning how to help others and
how to help myself.

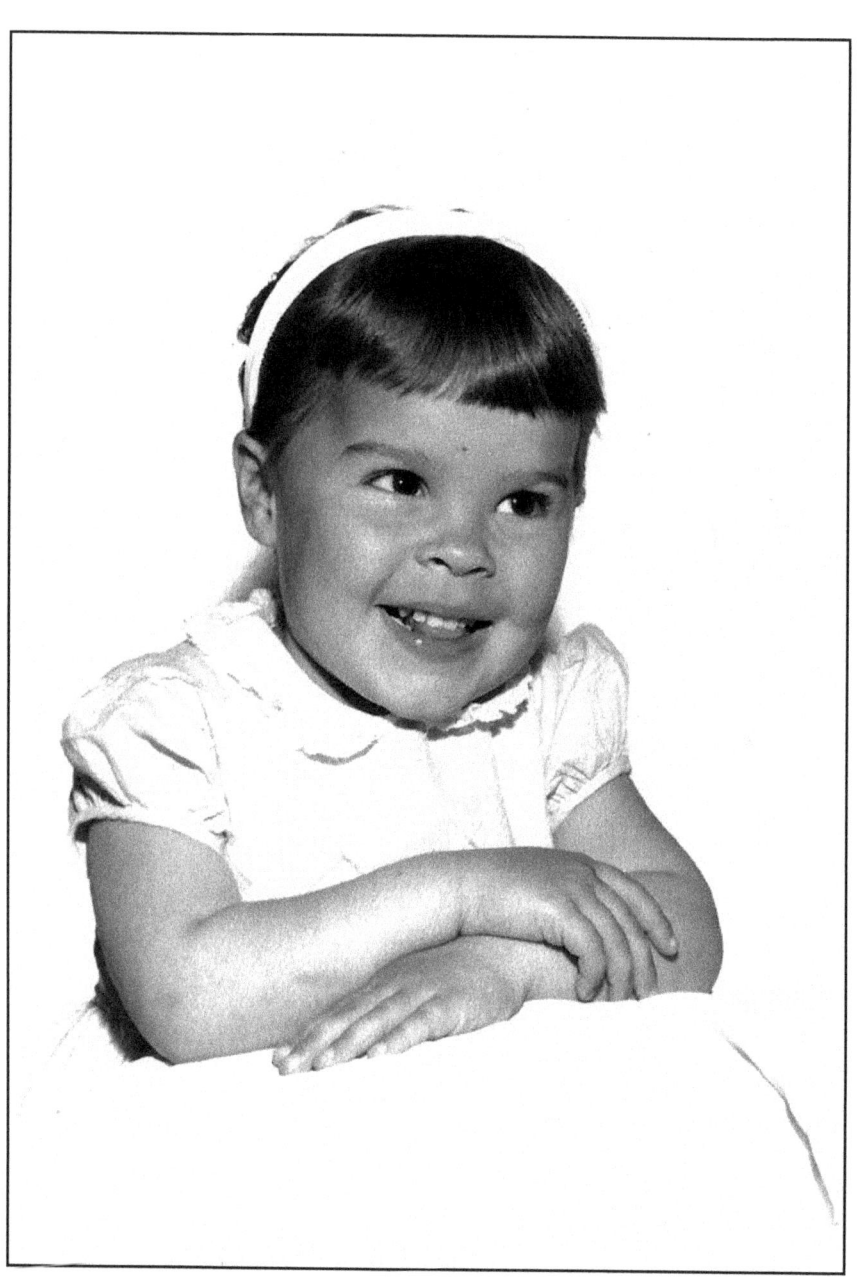

The Feldsparian Man

There once was a man of such great degree
that he knew everything of nature both wild and free.
But as well with this man was his love of the rock
the hard-clotted stuff, fixed, and all dotted as if it were mocked.
For he was the Feldsparian Man, the glue in between,
that kept that part of nature intact and pretty forever to be seen.
Right, the Feldsparian Man, you'd say, my fantasy.
But, no, he lives and is the glue of my life and dots my sheets
with me.

Somatization—No more—No thanks—
Forget the character defects today
Lord, I need to sleep
and I need to sleep steadily
Steadily
Steadily
Lift my anxiety from the hours
in which I need sleep
and place it into words
Talk about it.
Pray about the anxiety.
This week is for me
I need rest
I need your spirit to ease my anxiety
Now!

I feel no insecurity
I feel no great fear
Just the ongoing turmoil of my struggle
to let go and let God.
I'm always juggling, balancing,
diminishing, building,
thinking, thinking.
Help me to let go and experience
my flow, my bounce.
My vibrant energy in my life.

The Flu
Ill again
Elated again
Feeling hopeful
Still need strength
Still need to be still
Feeling trusting
Still need gratitude
Still need to pray
Feeling happy
Still need maturity
Still need you, God
Ill again
Elated again.

A bit of a change. A long list of things I love. Can be poetic, you know.
Puppies, satin, feathers, a beautiful complexion, nail polish along with
some nails, taxis, a soft breeze, losing weight, good food, a warm day,
warm rain, fur, snow, Tahoe, David Bowie, an old movie, waterbeds,
a good drug, a bottle of Scotch, champagne, fancy hotels, someone to
hug, a good cry, a good laugh, downers, small children, corner stores,
brick roads, close friends, pleasant dreams or fantasies, asleep or not,
Steve Marriott, faces, praying silently, over dramatizing,
Marilyn Monroe, snakeskin, cigarettes, pastries, green country,
old churches, deserts, jewelry, gloves, Rolls Royces and Jags, kisses,
chocolate, traveling, sleeping with someone you *really* like, cabins,
the South, New York, carnivals, horses, a fire in a room when there's
no heat, no food, no money and a storm outside, Rufus, Wags, Angel,
coming home after being away, parties, to dance, sing and act,
Led Zeppelin, Stevie Wonder, long slinky dresses, platforms, roses,
cussing, a rainbow, airports, concerts, backstage, cosmetics,
a pair of nylons that fit me, a new dress, omnibuses, the beach,
redwood, shiny black and white tile floors, tap dancing, butterflies,
good memories, good poetry, overwhelming excitement,
phone calls (good ones), unexpectedly a tan, White Shoulders perfume,
short hair on men, velvet, hard leather, flowers, good art, tapestries,
satin sheets, Mercedes, dinner shows, getting up early when you really *can*,
saunas, soccer, Canoe, camping once in a while, Chinese food,
Sausalito, imagination, parts of San Francisco, our canyon,
a good argument when you come out winning, Sammy Davis, Jr.,
Liza Minelli, *Midnight Cowboy*, boats, barbeques with family.

Traipsing desert stairs, dust in the nose, a blood rush
to the head—gasp!
Water, heat and rock—
rock smooth to the touch and spirit.
Not alone on this traipse.
So nice—stop
So nice stop—no, I need to believe this—stop
I really do.
It's simply nice to have a real—
 (real, meaning, I touch her— is she real?)
woman in my life.

Soft grains of gold, so fragile and light like an evening
melting into velvet dawn. Be gentle when you touch her hair.
Shades of olive and hazel, brilliant and shimmering
like a metallic bed of flowers.
Smile when you look into her eyes.
Silky colors of pink and lavender, like the fruit that makes
the rose wine.
Enjoy the taste of her lips.
Snowy feathered whiteness, like chiffon flowing in the
country wind.
Only a sensitive hand could feel her skin.
Let yourself gaze as she walks.
Can't help laughing with her as she talks.
Only imagine the dreams you've shared with her before she wakes.
Love, the ultimate, giving as the Goddess is the only kind she'll make.
From her the most beautiful colors, Oh, the shine, my God
how they glow.
She's my rainbow.
I love you.
I hate to go.

"Are you gathering up the pieces.
Have you had enough of mine?"
I mean after all the small experiences
we've shared as one,
can you really feel me now?
Actually touch me?
I soulfully love you.
Your helpless, hopeless heart begs
hello to sweet dreams.

Hello, nightmares.
Welcome, nightmares, though as a reality your existence is vague.
Love me, you say, and Oh, how passionately you can say it too.
You need. . .
The need of a warm fire when your spine quivers the word "Chill."
The need of true human touch, sensitive, gentle,
Let loose, caress, Caress . . . caressss.
Needing to say, "Mom, I feel ill today. May I rest in your bed?"
But the real need is, "Mom, lie beside me, hold me, never letting go."
Your love shows me the color of warmth—Red. I see the reddest of
all reds in your eyes.

Each Day is Never Long Enough

To feel every passing breeze flow
through my hair
To see every tree grow and blossom
into such figments of beauty
To watch every field and meadow waver
 in colors of green and gold
To hear every crash
of the ocean waves echo in my ears
To witness every sunrise and sunset
glazed a rusty orange
To realize that my life is worthwhile
and people in my life worth thinking of
All my days were never long enough
to experience these things

Friends

Hi Char,

I met your Leslie some 40 years ago in a nightclub there she was working in Studio City, CA. I was playing in the band and she was the waitress. We became good friends over time. My most memorable experience with Leslie was a trip we decided to take in the late '70s. After taking off from your home in Oakland we drove east to visit my grandparents in southeast Kansas. After driving through Nevada and into Utah, my car starting acting up, forcing us to stop in Salt Lake City for repairs. After spending the whole day there we decided to drive through the mountains at night to catch up the time we lost. Half way through the mountains we ran into a fierce blizzard with heavy winds blowing snow straight into the windshield making it impossible to see the road ahead. We had to choice but to stop in a little town, spend the night there and wait for the storm to clear. The next morning it was clear sailing for the rest of the way.

My grandparents, Floyd and Violette Hayes live on a farm outside of Iola, Kansas, which is 100 miles south of Kansas City. They loved having us visit them and treated Leslie like part of the family. The really cute thing was to watch Leslie and my grandmother talking face to face, not having to look up at the person they were talking to. You see, they were exactly the same height. After spending a few days we headed back to the west coast without incident. Leslie was so taken with the area and the people she met on the visit that she even went back on her own, living in Laurence where she took some classes at the University of Kansas. She would often go back to the farm and visit my grandparents on her own.

Leslie had an adventurous spirit, always looking for something new and interesting to do. I miss my friend and all the good times we had for all those years.

Bill Edwards

A Letter to the Gruendls

I just want to let all of you know what a great daughter and sister all of you had. She was my best friend till the end. I feel the last four years were the hardest for all of us. She was an incredible woman, a strong and compassionate loving soul. I will miss her.

She was like my sister in so many ways; we both have been through so much together in this lifetime. I can't even count how many times she called me when I was feeling down—her intuition was incredible. Our friendship was truly a gift from God! And we both knew that. We would talk about how blessed we were to have been able to spend this life together. My life will never be the same now, and I know yours will not either. I am sure we all have wonderful stories we could tell, and I do hope we get together soon to do so.

I am not sure what she told all of you, but she let me know that she wanted her ashes spread over Montclair Park. That is where Kevin Flynn first kissed her, and that's where we did have our first beer, and the stories go on from there.

Please keep in touch with me and let me know of your plans. I do have some great photos of us that I would love to share with everyone.

This is something read at my nephew Chad and my Dad's funerals:

Do not stand at my grave and weep
I am not there
I do not sleep
I am a thousand winds that flow
I am the diamond glints in the snow
I am the gentle autumn's rain
When you awaken in the morning rush
I am the swift uplifting rush
I am the soft stars that shine at night
Do not stand at my grave and cry
I am not there
I did not die

Love all of you,

Lynn

When I think of my dear friend Leslie, many emotions come to mind. She was an adventurer and a risk taker who had little fear. We both grew up in the Montclair hills, a place still abundant with raccoon, deer and vast beautiful trees. The little town of Montclair offered a community that was far from the dangers of the close-by bigger cities of Oakland and San Francisco. We both may have become naïve and trusting growing up in such a beautiful place. Leslie surely had confidence and was very outgoing. It was the time of the '60s where teenagers got around by hitchhiking. Music, drugs, and the peace of nature were focal points of many young kids, which included Leslie and me.

One incident with Leslie will always stand out in my mind. Leslie was a born leader and was more worldly than I was. We were both 15 years old, and Leslie had a great idea to see a music concert in San Francisco at the Fillmore. This was the hot spot to see the best well known bands at the time. "How will we get there?" I asked.

"We will hitchhike," Leslie replied nonchalantly.

OK, so we had figured it out! It was early evening, and my dad gave us a ride from the hills where we lived to the little town of Montclair, just a few miles away. Once there, we asked him to leave us at the park. I remember him asking, "So where are the people who are giving you a ride to the concert?"

I spoke up. "They are over there in the park waiting for us," and pointed to an unknown group of people. He wasn't quite sure of this, but assumed the best.

As soon as he was gone, Leslie and I stuck out our thumbs and a driver picked us up. How fortunate! He would give us a ride to San Francisco and would drop us off blocks away from the Fillmore. The Fillmore was located in a rundown area and not safe. However, when a concert was in town, the area was busy with cars filling the parking lots, and the streets were heavily loaded with people.

That evening was different. It was quiet. It was cold, empty and dark. There was no concert that night. We walked the sidewalk to get to a lighted, busier street and stopped at a cross light. A body stepped between us and grabbed each one of our arms firmly. It was a black man in his 30s or 40s, and he firmly said, "Keep walking, I have a gun and I will blow your heads off!" Both of us, too frightened to do anything, followed his command. Once across the street still holding firmly to our arms, he pulled us into the shadow of a building. "Give me your money!"

Leslie spoke up, "We don't have any." We really did, but it was hidden under our fancy dresses.

"How did you get here, then?"

"We hitchhiked," Leslie firmly said. Leslie was always good at talking her way out without giving any hesitation.

A police car must have seen us, so pulled up in front of us. "Hey, what's going on there? Are you girls all right?" he asked.

Too frightened of what our parents would say or do if they found out what we had done, Leslie replied, "We are all right."

"Are you sure?" the policeman asked again.

"Yes, he is helping us get to a taxi," Leslie answered.

"OK," he said, as he pulled away.

The black man, so thankful that we didn't turn him in, changed his demeanor. "What are you two girls doing in this neighborhood?! Don't you know that it's dangerous?"

We explained that the concert we had planned on going to must have been canceled and that we needed to get to a hotel to get a taxi back to Oakland. He became our advocate and protector.

"Well, I will walk you two to the hotel," he said.

"How are you going to pay for the taxi?" he questioned. Leslie, being quick-minded, again told him we would just "ditch" the driver.

So, the black man walked us to a hotel and we phoned a taxi. He waited with us and chatted with us like some old friend. The taxi finally came, and when we hopped in he waved us off safely.

It was getting late by the time the taxi drove us across the Bay Bridge to downtown Oakland. We had just enough money to pay for that ride and little left for going further. We got dropped off on Broadway in downtown and eventually hitchhiked again, back towards our quaint little town. Leslie was an adventurer with no fear. She could think on her toes and talk her way out of a situation with ease. She was ahead of her time with wanting to explore and experience life, which she did without hesitation.

Fortunately, along her journeys and that night, she must have had a guardian angel who protected us both. I am sure that angel is probably still at her side in heaven.

She was an amazing person and is greatly missed.

Diane Hawes Pereira

Leslie

Make a cup with your Hands.
Lower them to the sea.
You may hold the water but for a few moments. . .
As it rushes through the space of your fingers to escape,
Some absorbes through the pores to become part of you.

Like the water from the sea
You shall forever be Part of Me. . .

To my best friend,

I will love you always,

Lynn

It is a weird coincidence but last weekend my wife and youngest son drove to the old neighborhood and parked across from Vanvleet's old house and took a hike on Westridge and ended up back on top of Wilton, I had not been back in years to the place where us kids spent so many great times riding are bikes. I was looking out toward Saint Mary's and looked at this tree, it's a full grown pine tree now but at that moment I had a deja vu moment because I remember about 50 years ago Leslie and Lyn Mayer planted it, I have a weird memory for certain things I don't remember what I did yesterday but I remember that.

Danny

Family

I say I am a Christian, am I?
I try to see both sides, but struggle as I see my fear and
love entangle when they meet.
I love my brother, but I am afraid
of the pain he inflicts upon me.
Communication must meet halfway.
So I shall meet halfway then, but only if my brother does.
No, I have decided I shall meet halfway since my brother doesn't.

CHRISTMAS

As this special season begins to drift by, I am confused and
puzzled as to how to thank you. Words are about all I can
afford and a gift would be an understatement.

Your support throughout these recent years has kept me
secure and safe in a world I'd perceived as frightening.
My strength has increased, my outlook improved and
my attitude has never been better. My life is good. I
have you two to thank. You've been parents of the best
kind. I love you. Merry Christmas.

To Mom & Dad Xmas December '74

With lingering dreams of candy-coated love,
I slept in your quilted laps.

And that bubbly joy, silkened laced petticoats
fluttering parasols, your constant tickle.

Your pacifying stroke over my salty,
flushed and tear-drained eyes.

Times of forest green Sundays
and new strange
infancies in your sinless crib.

A childhood, a rare song of innocence.
Hidden from the naked eye,
padlocked from the human hand.

I am ingénue.
I have no ignorance. An infinite craving to know hounds me.
So carefree was I as I led my parade of idolatry, lust and
destructive moods.

I sat, my energy saturated
by some neighboring sponge.
And once new ideas stunned.
My destituted mind and heart, weary.

Then I recalled the nights
you've knelt and prayed, noticing,
your faces thin and pale.
"I found it hard to hide my tears you know,
felt ashamed, felt I'd let you down.
Well, I don't have much,
but what I've got is yours, except of course"
my platform shoes.
And we know our lives . . . will always differ a taste,
but that's why I love you.

And no flustering wind
could change a thing because
I love you.

Beau

Truth in life is clear.
My person is two years to come.
My soul will reflect through yours.
Will you have the insights?
Tabula rasa is the beginning of each new dawn.
Your smile is mine; without my smile, you cry.
Your cry frightens me.
Is it possible for you to always be happy?
For me? Please?

Beau T. and the butterfly. Running through the golden grain.
Beau T. and the butterfly. Play about the warm, green plains.
Beau T. and the butterfly. Always and forever friends.
Beau T. and the butterfly. Day of wonder and pretend.

Life is good
I feel held
I feel secure
The trail has filled me once again and my relation to
Beau is good—and I am good with Beau.
Yes—life is good.

Beau is gone—my heart aches. The joy and yearning
are both very, very, painful.

Cookie—my fuzzy little friend—you are a gift from Beau; and Beau is the best thing that ever happened to me. God, you did a beautiful job with him. I'm crying now because his perfect person brings overwhelming gratitude to my heart and to my soul. Oh, I found it! There's my soul. Its life begins with gratitude, with love and a deep thank you—to you, God.

Beau is a gorgeous, vibrant jewel, resting . . . then jolting, getting right out of its birthing rock. What a gorgeous jewel—pristine, shining out into the world. Take a good look, world, he's perfect, he's beautiful. He's in my life . . . Thank you.

January 24, 1981

Beau:
Someday when there is plenty of time, I'll be able to explain to you of all the crazy adventures your mother has lived through, none were as exciting or fulfilling as childbirth.
Of course, this is yours to experience with your mate someday. I hope you have full insight to really appreciate and be a part of the experience, for this is a rare trait among men.
Childhood is a time of innocence. Your expressions, Beau, your every smile, coo and giggle reassured me. You proved to me that there is such a thing as purity, simplicity and beauty. Could it be that every child born proves to us that God is still not discouraged with the human race.

June 12, 1981

Beau! I was never as happy in my life to see a baby boy step into my life. These first few months of your life are a little boring, but still enjoyable. Because of my impatience, I can't wait for you to grow up a little older, so we can play. I'm looking forward to sharing my childhood memories with you and teaching you things my father taught me as a child.

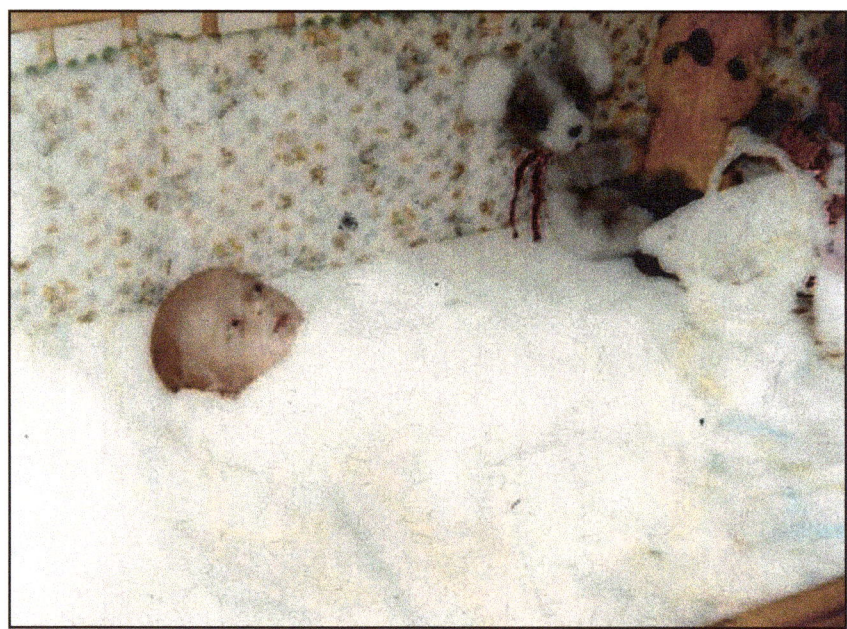

I Have Life

Shall I say, I have gone at dusk thru narrow streets
and watched the yellow smoke that crawls from the pipes
near lonely men in shirt sleeves leaning out of windows?
Watched my people grow in circles with minds of twisted rope and
feelings of silent seas?
Seen the sun rise in all my lovers' eyes and set in my torn, weary
heart?
Known the evenings, mornings, and afternoons
I have measured my life with coffee spoons, and cigarettes?
Traveled the world and all its reality, but trampled over make-believe,
and stumbled into myths?
This and so much more.
And shall I say it was all worth it? After all the falls, lovers, and cups
of coffee?
What I had, have, and will have?
My God—of course it was all worth it. I had it all the time and will
never lose it.
I have seen the bluest of the sky and tasted its tear of dew.
Felt the earth between my fingers and captured its beauty.
My soul has touched the soul of another and made love thru the
night with infinite fever.

Simplicity
I have life.

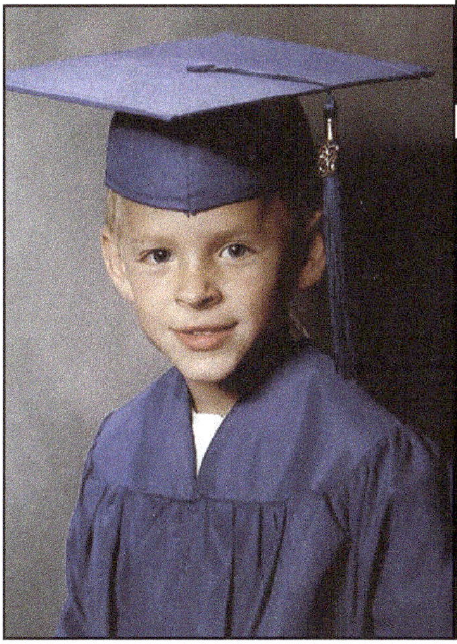

About the Editor, Charlotte Swanson Gruendl:

Charlotte was born in San Francisco, California, and grew up in Oakland. At age 16, while on a streetcar in San Francisco, she met the love of her life, Ray Gruendl, a Navy man, and she is still with him after 72 years. She became a real estate broker in the Bay Area, and she volunteered with charitable organizations while managing to raise five children. In 1989, she and her husband retired and moved to the Sierra community of Arnold, California. She was inspired to compile her daughter's creative writing after her daughter passed away in 2014. She discovered Leslie's journals, and was very touched by the beauty of her writing. She and her husband chose to share her writing with others and thought that it may provide insights and that her words would be beneficial to others. Char has an active life playing bridge, quilting, and spending time with her five grandsons, two great-grandchildren and many friends.

Leslie J. Tepper, Ph.D.
Clinical Psychology
595 East Colorado Boulevard
Pasadena, California 91101

Academic Background

1979 – 1982   Baccalaureate – Political Science – Cum Laude – California State University, Northridge, CA

1983 – 1985   Master of Science – Educational Psychology – California Lutheran College, Thousand Oaks, CA

1986 – 1991   Doctor of Philosophy – Clinical Psychology – California Graduate Institute, Los Angeles, CA

Dissertation Topic

A Psychological Model: Acquired Hearing Loss in Post-Lingual Adults. *Guest Lecturer, Emotional Components To Acquired Hearing Loss: Mission Community College, Sylmar, Ca, Shhh* (Self Help for Hearing Impaired Organization) Sherman Oaks, CA, Skilled nursing and retirement facilities throughout Southern California.

Licensure

Clinical Psychologist – State of California – License number PSY 1347 – August 1993

Psychotherapy Specializations

Depression, Anxiety and Personality Disorders
Alcohol/Chemically Dependent and Recovering Populations
PTSD/Critical Debriefing
Deaf, Hearing Impaired (sign Language Used)
Gay and Lesbian Populations
Severe and Persistently Mentally Ill
Individuals Diagnosed with HIV

Families/Couples
Group and Individual Psychotherapy
Adult Attention Deficit Disorder
Disability Evaluations

Publications and Presentations

Assessing The Efficacy Of An Inpatient Psychiatric Program, California Psychologist, April 1995, Vol. XXVII, no.3, Principal Author. Presented at the California Psychological Association's Annual Convention, 1995, in San Diego, California

The Outcome Evaluation And Program Development Team: A New Program Concept, Treatment Today, Summer Issue, 1995, Principal Author

Consumer Satisfaction Surveys: A Tool For Change, The Advocate – Newsletter of the National Alliance for the Mentally Ill, September/October, 1995. Principal Author. Presented at CASRA, California Association of Social Rehabilitation Agencies, November 1996. Presented survey development project results and conducted workshop on how to develop client satisfaction measures.

Can Quality Of Outpatient Treatment For Schizophrenia Be Assessed? Acknowledged. Principal Author – Alexander Young, M.D., *Journal of Psychiatry*, July, 1998

1997 – Facility participant in *LA County Epidemiology Study* – LA Health Services – *HIV Seroprevalence in Severe and Persistently Mentally Ill*. Collaborator for LA Metropolitan Medical Center. *Los Angeles County Mental Health Newsletter* – Acknowledged.

Prevalence Of Religious Coping In Severe And Persistently Mentally Ill. Two-year study completed and presented at the 2000 APA Convention in Washington, D.C. Published in *Psychiatric Services*, Vol.52, No.5, May 2001, Principal Author.

God As Reconstructive In Schizophrenia. Presented at the International Psychoanalytic Pre-Congress, Nice, France, July 2001. Published in the *International Psychoanalytic Studies Organization Journal,* Summer 2003 (Online), Author.

Religious Coping Of Those With Severe Mental Illness. Presented at the 2001 APA Convention, San Francisco, CA. *International Journal for the Psychology of Religion*, Vol.12, No.3, pp.161-175, 2002, Author.

Changes In Attitude Toward Religion In Those With Persistent Mental Illness. Presented at the 2002 APA Convention, San Francisco, CA. *Journal of Religion and Health*, Vol.41, No.2, Summer 2002, Author.

Organizations and Boards
1987 Scholarship recipient – American Women's Business Association
Member – American Psychological Association – Divisions 36 and 39
Member – National Alliance for the Mentally Ill
Member – Prescribing Psychologists Register
Member – Southern California Psychoanalytic Society

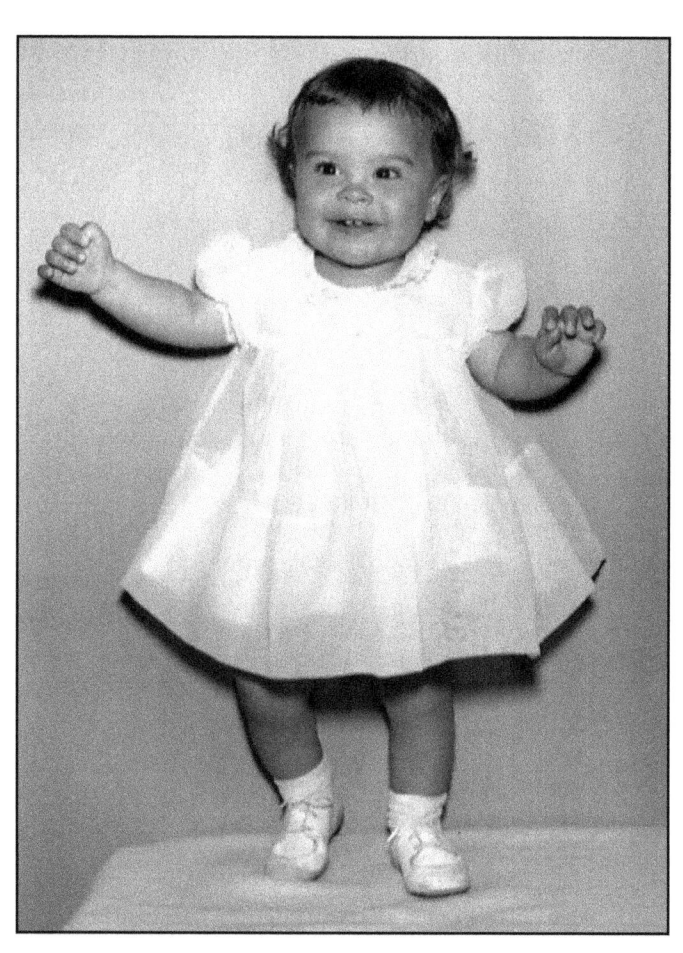

www.ingramcontent.com/pod-product-compliance
Lightning Source LLC
Chambersburg PA
CBHW051552010526
44118CB00022B/2674